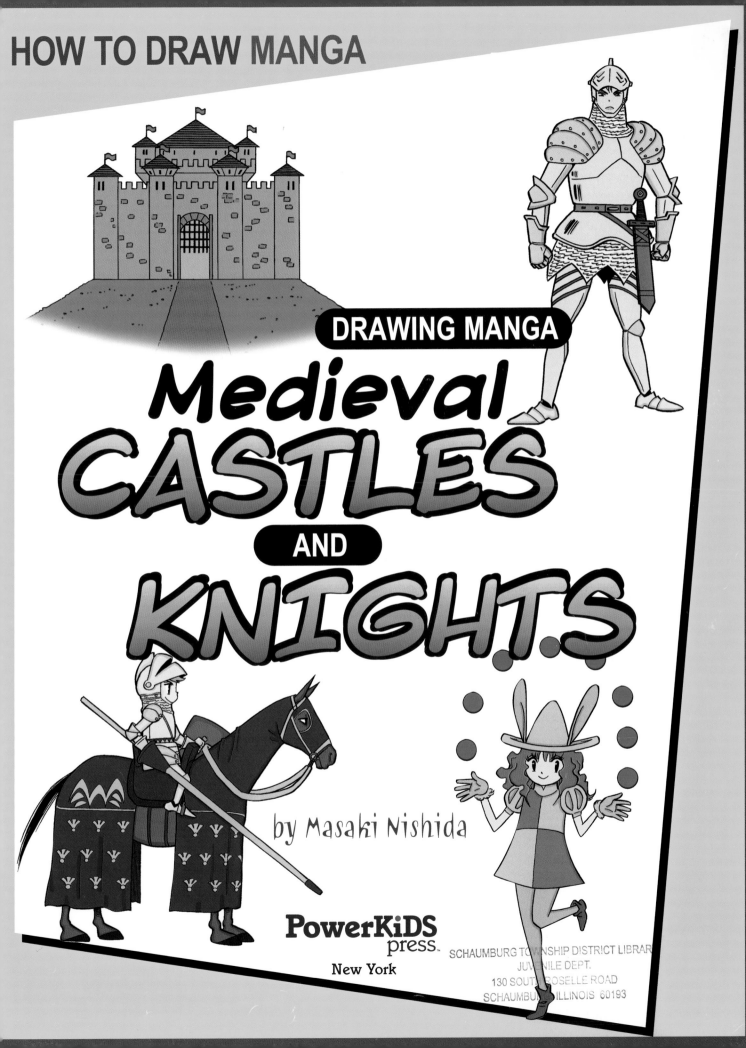

DRAWING MANGA

Medieval CASTLES AND KNIGHTS

by Masaki Nishida

PowerKiDS press™

New York

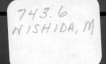

3 1257 01671 6762

Published in 2008 by The Rosen Publishing Group, Inc.
29 East 21st Street, New York, NY 10010

First Edition

American Editor: Victoria Hunter
Japanese Editorial: Ray Productions
Book Design: Erica Clendening
Coloring: Erica Clendening, Julio Gil, Thomas Somers, Gregory Tucker

Manga: Masaki Nishida

Library of Congress Cataloging-in-Publication Data

Nishida, Masaki, 1960-
  Drawing manga medieval castles and knights / Masaki Nishida.
    p. cm. \ (How to draw manga)
  Includes index.
  ISBN-13: 978-1-4042-3849-7 (library binding)
  ISBN-10: 1-4042-3849-2 (library binding)
 1. Knights and knighthood in art \Juvenile literature. 2. Castles in art \Juvenile literature. 3. Middle Ages in art \Juvenile literature. 4. Comic books, strips, etc. \Japan \Technique \Juvenile literature. 5. Cartooning \Technique \Juvenile literature. I. Title.
  NC1764.8.K55N57 2008
  741.5'1 \dc22

                          2007016376

Manufactured in the United States of America

CONTENTS

Learning About Manga

Hello, my name is Masaki. I am a manga artist who likes to draw many things. I have always loved reading and drawing manga and I have created all sorts of drawings about history, **adventure**, and even sports!

In this book my friend Sayomi and I will show you how to draw manga medieval castles and knights step-by-step. There's Sayomi on the right.

Manga has always been very **popular** among the Japanese. It is a **unique** Japanese art form that takes ideas from American **comic books**. Today, manga is popular all over the world and is enjoyed by many different kinds of people.

People like manga because of its interesting **combination** of pictures and **text**. The stories are easy to follow and **exciting** to read. We can create all sorts of adventures using manga. In this book we will draw eight important parts of the medieval world in the manga **style**. Let's go visit the manga medieval world!

The supplies that you will need to draw manga medieval castles and knights are:

- A **sketch** pad
- A pencil
- A pencil sharpener
- A ballpoint or a fine felt pen
- An eraser
- A ruler

Hi! My name is Sayomi. I'm very excited to learn how to draw the medieval world, aren't you?

This book will show you how to draw manga medieval castles and knights. It also contains short stories about a young knight's adventures.

You can use your manga drawing skills to recreate these stories. You can also use these stories as **inspiration** to come up with your own stories and **characters**. Anything is possible in the world of manga, now let's get drawing!

DRAWING A CASTLE EXTERIOR

The castle is the building where the lord, his family, and his knights lived in medieval times.

Now let's draw one.

1 First, draw a rectangle.

2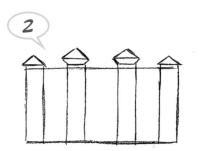
Draw four long rectangles and four triangles.

3
Add rectangles and triangles on top to give the castle *dimension*.

4
When you've finished with the rough drawing, add more details.

5
Ink the lines you'd like to keep.

6
Finally, you can add color and shading to your castle.

DRAWING AN
ARMORED KNIGHT

A knight is a strong **warrior** who guards the lord and the castle.

1
Draw an oval for the head.

2
Draw a rectangle and a trapezoid to start the **armor**.

3
Add circles and rectangles for the rest of the body.

4
Add details such as the face, helmet, and sword.

5
Ink the lines you'd like to keep. Erase any extra pencil lines.

6
Now color in your knight!

DRAWING A
JOUSTING KNIGHT

A joust is a **competition** in which knights compete in bravery and **technique**.

1 Draw an oval.

2 Draw another oval and two lines to make the horse's torso.

3 Add more lines and circles to complete the horse.

4 Now, add the knight using circles and rectangles.

5 Add the pole, helmet, and the horses's clothes.

6 Draw details and use ink over the lines you'd like to keep. Erase any extra pencil lines.

7 Color in your jousting knight!

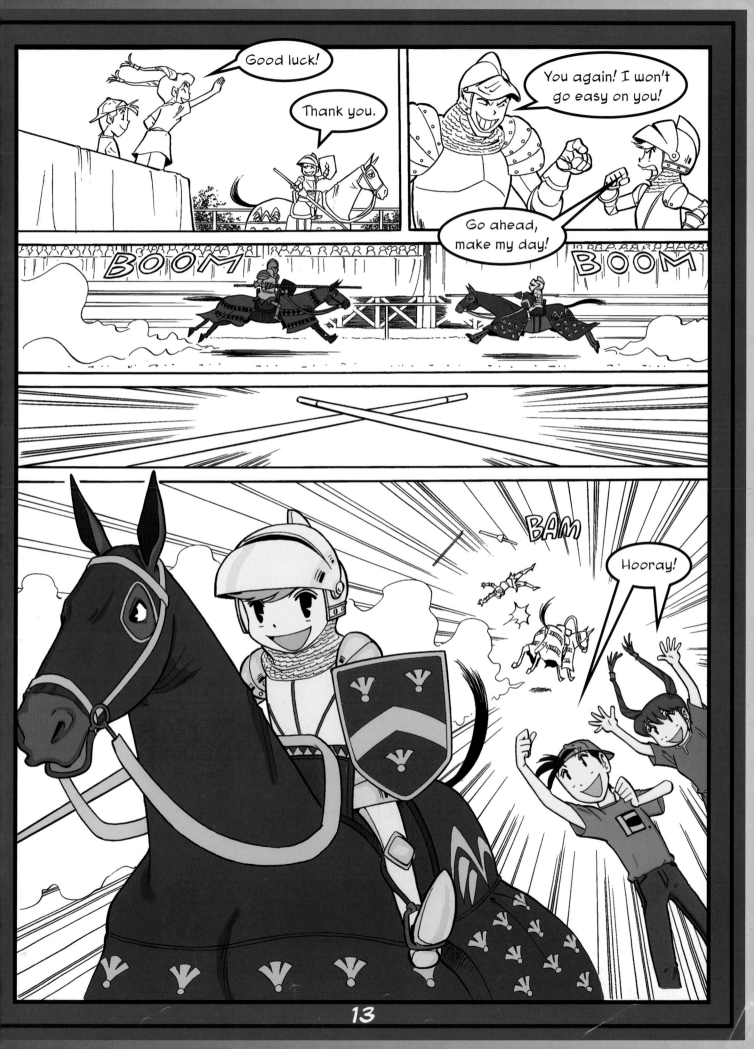

DRAWING A
CASTLE UNDER ATTACK

Oh no! It's an **attack** on the castle! Fight, knights, Fight!

Let's draw a castle being attacked!

1

Start by drawing a rectangle. Then draw a curve inside for the hill.

2

Draw rectangles for the castle and the knights.

3

Add the arms, swords, and the second **level** of the castle.

4

Add details, such as smoke, rocks, and the knights' clothing.

5

Ink the lines you'd like to keep.

6

Color and shade your drawing!

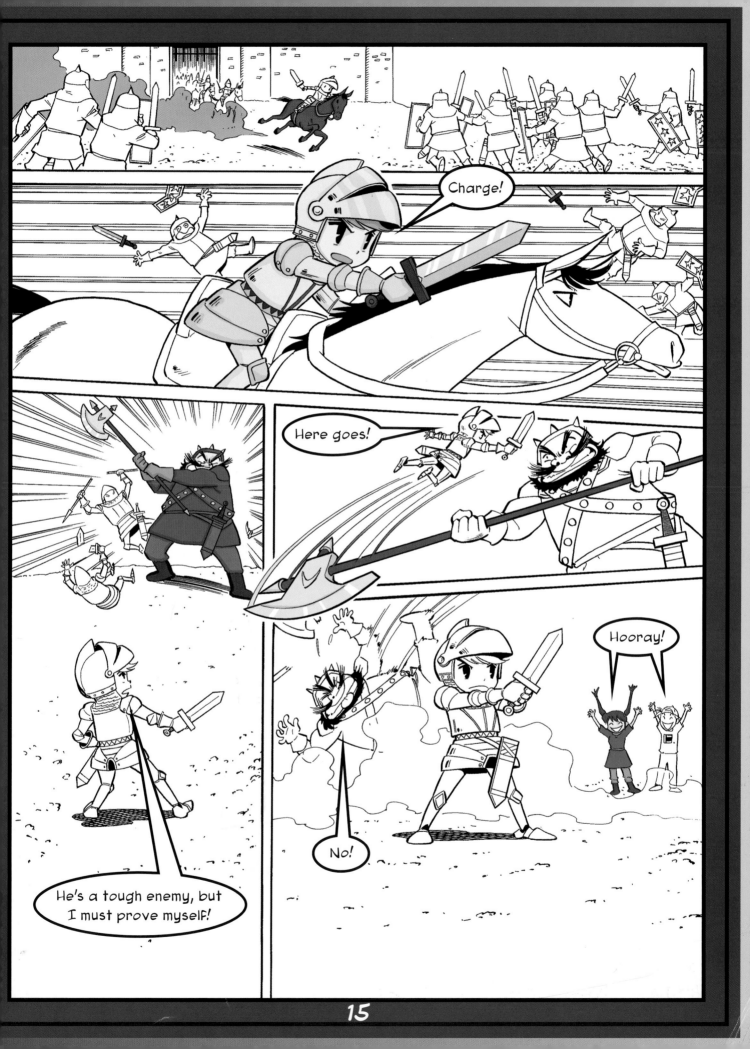

DRAWING A
PRINCESS

The princess is one of the most important characters in the medieval world.

That's right!

1 Draw a circle for the head.

Add a rectangle and trapezoid for the dress.

2

3 Add the crown, arms, and feet.

6

4 Draw details such as the eyes, *sash*, and the folds of the skirt.

5 Finish the detailing and ink over the lines you'd like to keep.

Add color and shading. Your princess will be beautiful!

DRAWING
MEDIEVAL WOMEN'S CLOTHING

Medieval women dressed up in many different ways.

Here are some examples of medieval women's clothing that you can learn to draw!

Ring

Brooch

Hat

GLOSSARY

adventure (ed-VEN-cher) An unusual or exciting thing to do.

armor (AR-mer) A type of uniform used in battle to help protect the body.

attack (uh-TAK) An act of trying to hurt someone or something.

characters (KER-ik-turz) Individuals in a story.

chivalry (SHIH-vul-ree) Noble qualities, such as courage, honor, and a readiness to help the weak and protect women.

combination (kahm-buh-NAY-shun) Something that is mixed or brought together.

comic books (KAH-mik BUHKS) Books with drawings that tell a story.

competition (kom-pih-TIH-shun) A game or test.

conquered (KON-kerd) Overcame something.

crest (KREST) The special seal of some person, family, or ruling body.

decorated (DEH-kuh-raytd) Added objects that make something prettier or more interesting.

dimension (duh-MEN-shun) The length, width, and height of an object.

exciting (ik-SYT-ing) Stirring up interest.

inspiration (in-spuh-RAY-shun) Powerful, moving guidance.

level (LEH-vul) How high something reaches.

popular (PAH-pyuh-lur) Liked by lots of people.

sash (SASH) A broad band worn around the waist.

shield (SHEELD) Anything used to guard a person.

sketch (SKECH) A quick drawing.

style (STYL) A particular manner or method in which an artwork is made.

sword (SORD) A weapon with a long, sharp blade.

symbol (SIM-bul) An object or a picture that stands for something else.

technique (tek-NEEK) A method or way of bringing about a desired result in a science, an art, a sport, or a profession.

text (TEKST) The words in a piece of writing.

unique (yoo-NEEK) One of a kind.

warrior (WAR-yur) A person who fights in a war.

All About the Medieval World!

Castle Exterior
The backdrop of most medieval stories. A place for banquets, wars, and royal families.

Armored Knight
One of the main players in a medieval adventure. He can be the hero or the villain!

Jousting Knight
An important character when adding action to your medieval tale.

Princess
A special character in a medieval story. She can be the heroine, the prisoner, or even the evildoer!

Castle Under Attack
A common scene in medieval adventures. Battles often took place at castles.

Medieval Jester
Most often seen at a medieval banquet to entertain the royal family and guests.

INDEX